# Animals
## and
# Plants

by Shirley Horton

# Animals Live in Different Habitats

Animals live in different places. Their body parts help them.

Polar bears can live in very cold places. They have fur. Fur helps keep them warm.

These animals help each other. Shrimp do not see very well. They can feel with their **antennae.** The shrimp feel the tails of the fish. The fish lead the shrimp.

Goby fish

Snapping shrimp

# Animals Get Food

Animals use their body parts to get food. Some birds use beaks to eat. Some bird beaks can tear meat. Some bird beaks can open seeds and nuts. Animal teeth can break nuts too.

**Hawk**

Bears catch fish to eat. They use their claws and teeth. Zebras eat grass. Their flat teeth help them bite and chew.

# Animals Stay Safe

Animals have different ways to stay safe. The colors and shapes of animals can protect them. **Camouflage** is a color or shape. It makes animals hard to see.

**This toad uses camouflage.**

**Praying mantis**

This insect is hard to see. It looks like a plant stem with a leaf. Camouflage helps it hide from other animals. Camouflage also helps it get food.

# Hiding in the Water

This big snake hides under water. Its nose and eyes are on top of the water. It waits for animals that come near the water. Then it pulls them in. The animals are its food.

# Animals Warn of Danger

A rabbit can tell other rabbits that there is danger. It hits its back foot on the ground.

A prairie dog can tell other prairie dogs that there is danger too. It makes a loud bark.

**Prairie dogs**

# Plant Parts

Plants are living things too. They have parts that help them live.

The **roots** take in water for the plant.

The **flower** makes seeds.

The **stem** takes water from the roots up to the rest of the plant.

The **leaf** makes food for the plant.

# Plants in Different Habitats

Plants live in different places. Plants need light from the Sun to grow. This plant lives in a dark rain forest. The big leaves can take in lots of light for the plant.

**Heliconia**

Plants need water to grow. This plant lives in a desert. The desert does not have much water. The little leaves help keep water inside the plant.

**Ocotillo**

13

# Plants Stay Safe

Plants have many ways to stay safe. Some plants have spines or thorns. Spines and thorns can hurt animals. Animals do not want to eat these plants. Other plants have a bad taste or smell. That keeps animals away too.

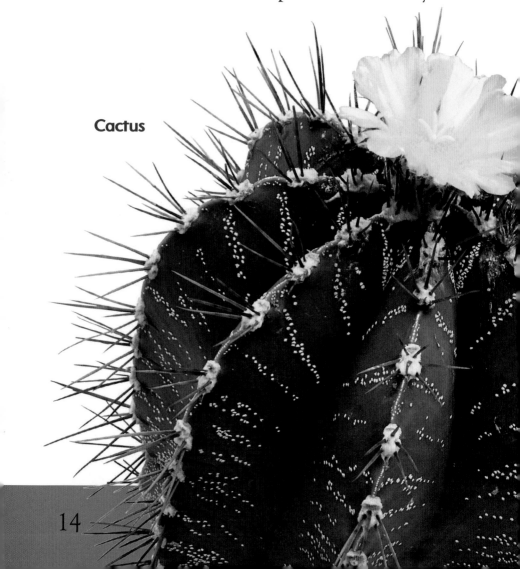

**Cactus**

Some plants use camouflage like animals do. Some plants look like the ground. They are hard to find. They stay safe.

Now you know a lot about parts of animals and plants. What are some parts that keep them safe? What are some parts that help them get food?

# Glossary

**antennae**    feelers an animal uses to feel, smell, and taste

**camouflage**    a color or shape that makes a plant or an animal hard to see

**flower**    the part of the plant that makes seeds

**leaf**    the part of the plant that makes food

**root**    the part of the plant that takes in water

**stem**    the part of the plant that moves water around the plant